A [
POEMS TO THE DIVINE
(that exists in us all)

Lucia Bunge Guerrico

Gracias, gracias, gracias.

Yoga has been around for nearly 5000 years. If you meditate or practice yoga today, you are a modern yogi.

CONTENTS

PROLOGUE

A great teacher said to me and a group of other yogis in a silent yoga hall somewhere in paradise: "Reading sacred texts and poetry before meditation can change everything." And it did. That moment at Hridaya Yoga School in Mazunte, Mexico was when my journey with divine Poetry began. Daniel Ladinsky's "Love Poems from God," with works of Hafiz, Rumi, Rabia, and other saints, sank deep into my soul. I'd read a couple of pages after and before meditation, before bed, as soon as I woke up, or whenever my soul needed a little taste of bliss. As soon as I finished this book, I continued to read the works of Hafiz and Rumi.

I thought I had an understanding of

divinity before then, but there was
something about reading the art of
illuminated beings that kissed my soul
so deeply, and allowed me to become
more aware of divinity all around me.

This collection of poems are all fruits
of meditation. Like a divine download, the
words came. Since I was meditating, I had
to let go of them in the moment, but as
soon as the gong from my meditation
timer sounded... a pen was in my hand.
Usually, I'd remember the exact words.

I didn't really intend to make a book
out of this. "Who reads poetry anymore
anyways?" I said to myself. However, I let
the divine act through my fingers as
much as I could The divine downloaded
the words into my conscious mind, then
they made their way onto my journal and

somehow the words that were first adorning my personal ruled pages made way into my computer and alas, your eyes are now taking them in.

Funny how the divinity in me and the divinity in you find union in these lines once more.

I am deeply honored.

Perhaps you'll read these pages before meditation, or before bed; Or read them aloud at the end of a yoga class, or whenever your soul would like a sweet taste of pure divine bliss. Maybe you'll even share them with a friend or two.

If you let yourself become softer and let these words sink in, these pages might even help you towards your journey of love and enlightenment.

When reading these words, don't try

to rush through. Instead, savor them. Enjoy each bite. And you don't have to keep reading once you're full. Maybe wait until you feel hungry again.

Breathe in
Breathe out

I am god

I am god
& so are you
please my beloved
please
let it
shine
through

God took me out dancing

God took me out dancing
I sang with the stars
slow danced with the Oceans
and made love with galaxies
I sang the sound of Creation
and felt my vocal chords vibrate
the big bang occurred

Oh, we had great fun
I didn't even have to dress up
I just wore the night sky
as my gown
the moon was my necklace
Leo and Cancer were my earrings

God took me out dancing
oh, we have great fun
every time I close my eyes
and feel the Universe within
I see him on the dance floor
calling me over
he wants me to dance with him again

Connect to your heart center

To love someone

To love someone
Is to witness
The beauty
Of the entire universe
In another's smile

There once was a Buddha
some call it a God
others call it a deity
some don't see through mind fog

It has millions of eyes
that open and close
some dying, some birthing
they have hearts, brains and nose

This buddha connected
to creatures by holes
in the heart of their brains
as deep as you go

She feels what they feel
he hears what they hear
all at once and forever
the love and the fear

These creatures or beings
when clear they realize
they're all part of this god
with the billions of eyes

There once was a Buddha

Connect to your source

Different expressions
yet one and the same
reflections and mirrors
all playing a game

The game is called life
and the goal is to live
connect with each other
to love and to give

We may harness the power
if we go deep within
or in the eyes of our neighbor
when we see great Kuan Yin*

So dive in compassion
diving out, and within
for this God lives inside us
and we live inside him

see appendix

Dear beloved

Dear beloved
may it be that you send me
these wounds
because you know
the strength of my faith
and you wish for me
to strengthen it
a little more

The eternal moment

The eternal moment
I said to the Universe:
"take me to the right place!
please god."

And God answered:
"be here now.
this moment is eternal."

Ask yourself the question: Who am I?

Let go
and the lines are erased
everything merges

As I sat here
I turned into a tree
nothing to do
just everything to be

I let it shine through me
for I am it all
and it is all me

Let Go

Samadhi

Samadhi*
is like melting
into the cosmos
through cracks

Drip by drip
into an Ocean
of nothingness

Do nothing
and gravity
will do the job

see appendix

Focus your attention on the space between
inhales and exhales

The whole Universe
exists in a second
and the big bang occurred thrice
as I drew in a breath

Time is a beautiful song
and we sing it together
sitting under the stars
let's play to this beat
as it goes on forever

And sing at the top of our lungs
or maybe a whisper

Draw in a breath
to prepare
the big bang might
happen again

The whole universe

The Sun kissed me today
at sunset
I felt his tenderness
and grace
in my heart

I forgot how to blink
afraid I'd miss out on anything
I wanted to take it all in
to miss nothing

The birds had the same thought
for we are all the same
we are all you
my beloved

We posed our best poses
and flapped our wings

So the sun might notice
once more
as the wind pushed us
into the sky

The sun kissed me today

There is something very sacred about
breathing into your heart space

Today I achieved

Today I achieved
Enlightenment
As I was doing the dishes
hopefully
I can stay in samadhi*
as I hop in the shower

see appendix

The beauty of silence

The beauty of silence
is that
in what you don't say
some things stand out

And those words might be
of the truest value

In what you withhold
you may find the treasures
and the voice of God

Focus on the space between thoughts and with each breath... allow it to expand

When in meditation

When in meditation
as Samsaric* thoughts
of others appear
dive into their self as well

See life from their eyes
feel touch through their pores
draw their smile on your face

And everything
you may offer
in devotion
to the divine

see appendix

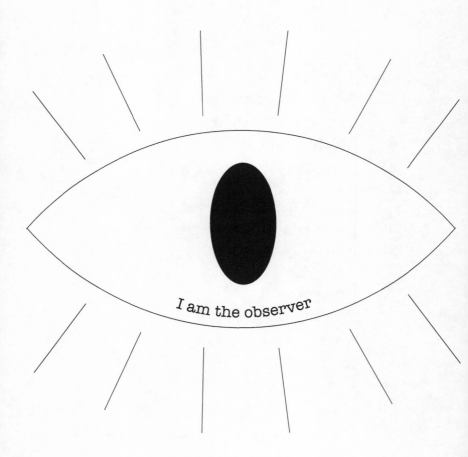

I am the observer

Who are you

Who are you
ask yourself
who am I
beyond the names
and the stories

In time much has changed
your body
your personality
surroundings
friends
yet the self
has always been

What is that self
that observes
and enjoys
and mourns
and sees
the story of your life
play out

The observer
we share
with all living things
and who knows
maybe even the non living

The space between thoughts is the source
where the whole Universe comes from

"Non violence"

"Non violence"
I remind myself

Does that then mean
that I must be gentle
with my ego
as well?

The drinks we drink

The drinks we drink
and the food we eat
by the divine magic
some may call science
turns into our body

Today
in my cup of hot chocolate
time was an illusion
and I saw myself smiling back
and felt me
going down my own throat

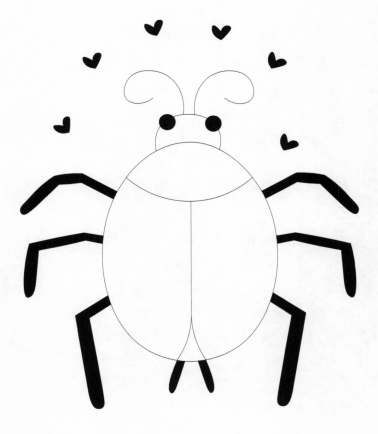

The ego

The ego
is like a cockroach
I thought
you think it is dead
and you must kill it again
and then
and then
I realized
there was no way to express those
words with love
and my highest self whispered
ahimsa,
non violence
my dear

Can you make your next breath sacred,
gentle?

Behind the noise

Behind the noise
there is silence
behind the clouds
there is sky
behind the mind
there is soul
behind division
there is oneness

Write your story

Write your story
play your role
in this Samsaric*
come and go

Close your eyes
repeat again
that conversation
with your friend
You're in a cycle
is there an end?

And then you realize
just be in flow
Be like the breath
just let it go

see appendix

This moment is infinite

We are all

We are all
but the self
everlasting
everythingness

Yet there is such pleasure
in the chuckles
with a dear friend
about the silliness
of the human experience

There is divinity
in the humanity
that we are
and are not
and God laughs with us too

It is in our nature to create,
my love

Create humans
create art
create love

Thank you
for making me
in your image my dear

And giving me these hands
that hold the power
to create
a whole galaxy

And express
through my fingers
the creative power
of the soul

It is in our nature to create

Thoughts are like clouds, breath is like the wind. When a thought comes up and it gets cloudy; with an exhale you can blow it away to far away lands.

I've been doing everything like it's for God

I've been doing everything
like it's for God

I wash her dishes
and chew her food
I take out her trash
and walk her around

And remind her often
what incredible work
she has done
with this experience

The divine

The divine
is a pure
highly addictive
nectar
it awakens passion
and force
and drive
maybe you will even be
in bed
so high
on the nectar
some people might even say
you are having too much of it
your eyes will twinkle
you cannot cease to think of it
your heart will pour out
into everything
you do
you will devote it all
if you just take the first sip
and the first real feel
I promise
you will become a junkie
and will only be able to satiate
your thirst in divine silence
and the royal darkness
behind closed eyelids

Breathe in
Breathe out

Your mind and body

Your mind and body
Are but a drop
In the vast ocean

Of consciousness
would not a drop

Feel more happy
and powerful
and full
if it realized
it was the Ocean

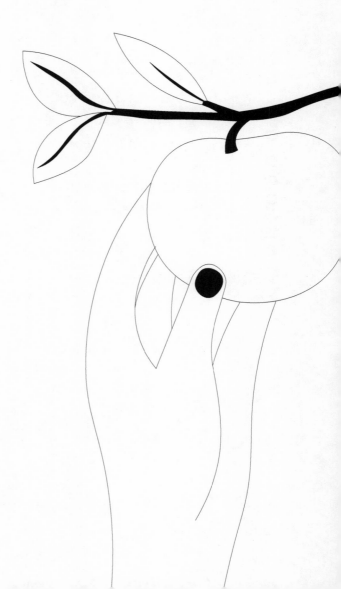

I feel the whole Universe

I feel the whole Universe
dancing to my heartbeat
and drinking from my breath
in every cell
of my loving
wise body

The silence is key

The silence is key
and the heart
feels like home
ask yourself the question
who am I
and listen
to your heart
for its loving
and silent
response

Connect to your heart center

How magical

How magical
to think
every beauty
you have ever beheld
exists in the pure
potentiality
that sits
on the inside
of your eyelids

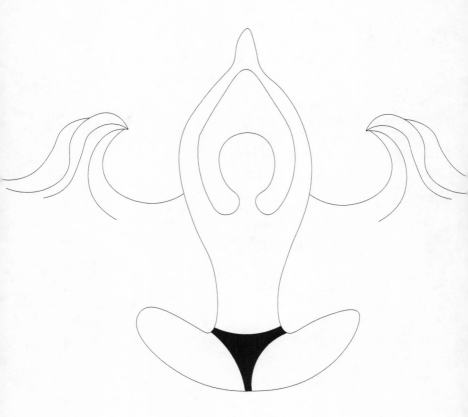

Take your pain

Take your pain
and meditate it away

Take the pain
of everyone you love
and meditate it away

Take the pain of everyone
you have crossed paths with
and meditate it away

Take the pain
of everyone
you will never know of
and meditate it away

Somehow
in overcoming
the pain
there is pure love

Connect to your source

Come lay with me

Come lay with me
dear God
squish me with your warmth
till you and I
are merged together
forever
in this eternal
bliss
of union

The longing

The longing
for a moment not to end
stems from the need
to be present

When you fall
in love
with the divinity
in the space
between breaths

Time ceases
to matter
and exist

To make sweet love
with the divine
in the center
of your chest
a little to the right

To lose yourself
in everythingness
to be completely
present
awake
in love

It's like waking up
to the sweet skin
of your lover
and knowing
that this moment
is eternal

To make sweet love

Ask yourself the question: Who am I?

God likes to laugh

God likes to laugh
amusedly at her own jokes

If you listen closely
you can hear her
and her smile
undoubtedly
lights up your face
and cures anyone who listens

See
look at you
you're smiling
in her grace

THE
PRESENT
MOMENT

Any time desire appears

Any time
desire appears
I must remember
what I am truly seeking
is being here
now

I am thirsty
for the present
and in my breath
I find my holy drink

Focus your attention on the space between
inhales and exhales

I am drunk

I am drunk
in love
with you
my dear cosmos

You beat inside
each cell in my body
and adorn with holy light
the palms of my hands

By what strange miracle
could I
so often forget
that I am a dancing
quantum soup
of you
my dear

Dear beloved Universe

Dear beloved
Universe,
I see you
in the eyes
of a stranger
that smiles
and passes by

Hopefully they too
saw you
in me
swimming naked
in the pool
of my brown eyes

There is something very sacred about
breathing into your heart space

God take from me

"God take from me
everything
that keeps me from you"

Careful with this prayer
for it is powerful
and sniffs out your fears

Yet it may bring you
the happiness
of the entire Universe

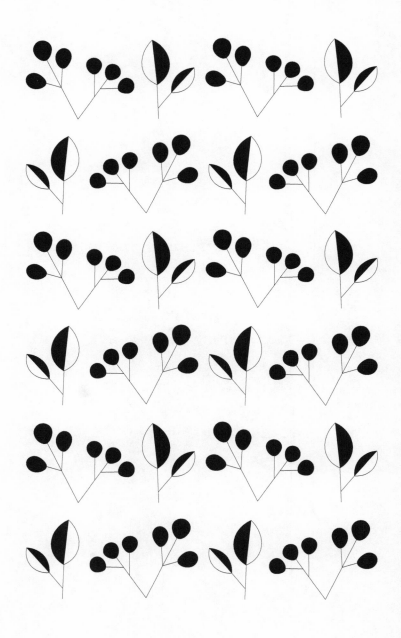

Once

Once
a witch told a dear friend
dogs do not have a soul

Maybe she needs to sit
with her heart
a bit more

So God whispers
in her ear with kindness
dog spelled backwards
is God my dear

Focus on the space between thoughts and with each breath... allow it to expand

Stars and fertile lands

Stars
and fertile lands
lovers
and figs
oceans
and heavens
birds flying
and kisses

All this is what I feel
in the stillness of my heart
yet i have not
even left my room
this morning
or turned on the light

I ask myself
who am i
and the universe whispers
"You are me
and I am lucky
to be you"

If you sit still enough

If you sit still
and stay with your heart
for a while
frequently enough
I assure you
you may discover
the treasures
of the entire cosmos

It glitters
and gleams
like the ocean
at sunset

Or a pond or a river
that is showing off
dancing in front of the Sun
and in front of your eyes

So hopefully
you might notice
her dance

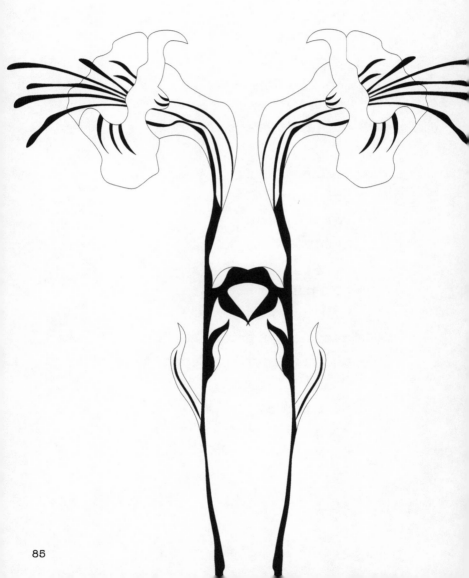

Today

Today
I talked to my food
I said to the food-God
inside my fig

Dear God
you really outdid yourself
with this fig
it tastes like heaven
she even looks
like a uterus to me

And the God inside
me replied
"Thank you"

And now that I think of it
I added
you really outdid yourself
with my uterus too
I bet it's as sweet
as this dear fig

Our thoughts
compared to our highest self
are like
a child
we must look at them
with compassion
love
and amusement
but not take what they say
too seriously

Instead focus more
on how they feel

And understand
that the true magic
and the most
undeniable truths
take place
in the occasional
beautiful
silence
of the here and now

Our thoughts

The space between thoughts is the source
where the whole Universe comes from

For years

For years
I loved so deeply
I thought
and wept
at the thought of loss

Many faces
different names
now I understand
I have always been
crazy in love
with you
my beloved

Crazy in love
with me
my many faces
and different names

God laughs

God laughs
and loves
and dances
and cries cursing
her lovers name

And lives
the human experience
and marvels
at the gleam
in your eyes

So near
and intimate
and far
and infinite

Can you make your next breath sacred, gentle?

Oh beloved

Oh beloved
amor mío
I searched in many lovers
for a love
that was unconditional
passionate
eternal

I knew it existed
no wonder
now I know
I was thirsty
for you

The flight of a bird

The flight of a bird
the sunset at sea
a friend's pretty eyes
strangers courting
lovers who walk
hand in hand

How beautiful we are my love

How beautiful

We are

This moment is infinite

The Universe

The Universe
feels happy
lucky
blessed
inspired
to be here now

The God
and Goddess in us
that we are
That "I am"
is blissful
loving
eternal

We are here
and now
and forever

In love
with all
that is

Do everything

Do everything
as if you were doing it
for God herself
that sweet
awareness
surrender
devotion
love

This can make
making your bed
in the morning
a holy experience

Remember my dear
every act
in this life
you're doing it for
God herself

Go ahead
try it out
as you breathe your
next breath
for her
and feel the love
settle in

Thoughts are like clouds, breath is like the wind. When a thought comes up and it gets cloudy; with an exhale you can blow it away to far away lands. *

I understand
why they go
into silence
for years with you
my love

Sometimes I play
the game we humans play
of I am this
and you are that

I understand

But I come back
to you
and to me
as I close my eyes

I come back to you
as I see you
in the eyes of another
or in the song
of their voice

I often play the game
we humans play
of you are this
and I am that
but in my heart
I know it's just pretend

I wish to be

I wish to be
Saint
holy
divine

My soul yearns
for that passion
that love
not that titles matter

Just merely
for the closeness
to God
that it entails

And what I wish for
I simply am

Lucia Bunge Guerrico

When God is let inside

When God
is let inside
fear can be blown out
like a weak
burning candle

For fear
is not but
the absence of love

106

Breathe in
Breathe out

When the dog bit me

When the dog bit me
somehow
it bestowed
a seed of enlightenment

It happened while I was praying
it could only be holy

In that moment
to God I gave my thanks

If I am everything
because everything is God
I am the Dog
so I bit myself

Sometime before
I had been speaking of animals as
enlightened beings
I could not help but laugh now

If Jesus bit you
or Mother Teresa
or Ghandi
first, you'd probably be mad
and frankly shocked

But then
would you not laugh?
would you not be deeply honored
you had lived to tell the story?

Thank you blessed creature
for you have freed
my soul

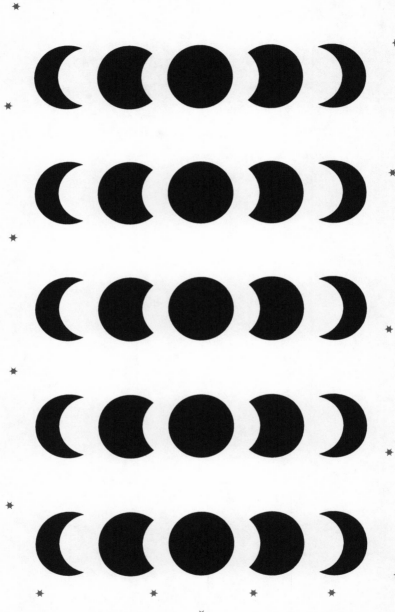

Devotion has brought

Devotion has brought
an unexpected gift
suddenly I know
that no matter
what happens
it's bringing me closer
to the beloved

Connect to your heart center

Never turn away a meal

Never turn away a meal
that was made for you
by someone that loves you
for it is love
in its purest form

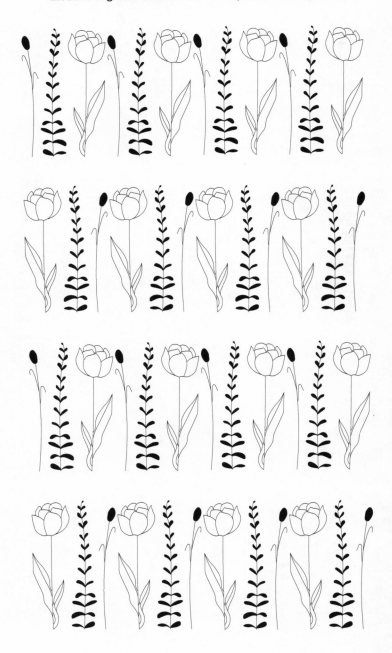

At times
a thought comes up
in the form of a beautiful poem
it comes straight from source

I feel it
as it conjures
and wonders me
with its beauty

My hands are only the vessel
yet the busyness of life
can sometimes
distract me
from the divine honor
of writing down these holy words

And so God asks me
for quietness
and solitude
and intimacy
with creation's
holy fire

At times a thought comes up

Connect to your source

When I am distracted
or forget my pen
and the poem dissolves again
into nothingness
and forget

I wonder
if it is gone forever
but if I trust it
and sit still

It will come back
for God
is loving like a child
and just wants
our love
and our attention

I would tell my younger self

I would tell my younger self
it's a journey
enjoy the ride

You are powerful
and divine
and beautiful

The depth of love
that you are seeking
outside
you can only find
within yourself

Passionate
deep
everlasting
it is here
now

And maybe
in my last breath
when my body and mind
surrender
to infinity
I will smile and say with God

Now I understand
it was all
part of the lesson

God has no gender

God has no gender
but I am a woman see
so I am
tempted
to call her she
to feel her close to me

Ask yourself the question: Who am I?

Dreams are powerful teachers

Dreams are powerful teachers
you are the dreamer
and you are also the dream

Some people like to lucid dream
and take control of their dreamland

This can be good fun
but sometimes
I also like to
sit back
and take the companion seat
to see where my dreamland will take me

You might even hear me saying
well that was a crazy dream
as if it was something I hadn't conjured

you are the dreamer,
and you are also the dream

But I am only
referring
to me

You may tell yourself
this life's crazy
and then remember
it is all part
of a crazy dream

And maybe
who knows
maybe
you'll remember
you can always lucid dream

Focus your attention on the space between
inhales and exhales

In a world where

In a world where
hate
and war
and division
are at large
the best thing you can do
is catch
a case of
Peace
so severe
it becomes contagious

That thing
that's bothering you
dive into it
naked
see how it feels

Let it steep in
sit with the pain
let it be
maybe even marvel
at it's beauty

That thing

What is a rose
without its thorns
what is a soup
without its spices

What is life
without unexpected turns
that we are meant
to get past

There is something very sacred about
breathing into your heart space

That thing
that's bothering you
swim in it
with your naked soul

For there is divine grace
in feeling
the pain
that's where the fun begins

Bliss

Bliss
tastes like
a warm hug
or waking up well rested
in the arms of your lover

Bliss tastes like
loving support
and the feeling
of falling in love

Bliss tastes like
deep breaths
and oneness
with the heart

Oh beloved
if they knew
what bliss tastes like
they would not live
a second more
without your embrace

Devote it all

Devote it all
my dear
devote the love
devote the pain
devote the stories
devote the passion
devote the heartbreak

For life is just
a story
and for the universe
we play our role

In devotion
there is surrender
and in surrender
we find the light

Appendix : Glossary of Terms

page 14 Kuan Yin:

Kuan Yin, also known as Guanyin or
Avalokiteshvara, is a bodhisattva of
compassion and mercy in East Asian
Buddhism, revered for her ability to
alleviate suffering and grant blessings.
She is also know as the Goddess
of compassion.

page 22&28 Samadhi:

Samadhi or enlightenment is a state of
intense concentration achieved through
meditation, where the mind becomes still
and focused, leading to spiritual insight
and union with the divine.

page 32&44 Samsaric:

Samsaric comes from the word Samsara
which refers to the cycle of birth, death,
and rebirth in Hinduism, Buddhism, and
ainism, representing the continuous cycle
of existence. It can also be used to point at
everyday life affairs.

Lucia Bunge Guerrico is originally from Argentina and was raised in the United States, the Dominican Republic, and Argentina, making her bilingual in English and Spanish.

She is licensed in Clinical Psychology from UCE University in the Dominican Republic. She has wanted to be a writer since she was old enough to know what being a writer was.

She is also a tarot card reader, as well as a yoga and fitness instructor.

Lucia Bunge Guerrico is passionate about helping others become the happiest and best versions of themselves.

Her journey with yoga and meditation began when she was 16 years old and started practicing Ashtanga yoga in Tucumán, Argentina. She used to wake up at 5 a.m. before school to fit in her meditation practice.

Her first spiritual experience occurred at the end of a very intense yoga class. She was in Savasana, a pose dedicated to recovery and meditation, in a deep meditative state, and she remembers thinking, 'Wow, this is God and it's inside me.'

The modern yogi also enjoys reading, drawing, singing, leading kirtans (devotional music circles), traveling the world, cooking, spending time outdoors, and surfing.

This is her first published work, with many more to come.

Lucia currently lives in sunny San Diego, CA, USA.

Made in the USA
Columbia, SC
21 June 2024